Explore!

NORMANS

Izzi Howell

WAYLAND
www.waylandbooks.co.uk

First published in Great Britain in 2016 by Wayland

Copyright © Wayland, 2016

ISBN 978 1 5263 0061 4
10 9 8 7 6 5 4 3 2 1

Wayland
An imprint of Hachette Children's Group
Part of Hodder & Stoughton
Carmelite House
50 Victoria Embankment
London EC4Y 0DZ

An Hachette UK Company
www.hachette.co.uk
www.hachettechildrens.co.uk

A catalogue record for this title is available from the
British Library

Printed and bound in China

Produced for Wayland by
White-Thomson Publishing Ltd
www.wtpub.co.uk

Editor: Izzi Howell
Designer: Clare Nicholas
Picture researcher: Izzi Howell
Illustrations: Julian Baker
Wayland editor: Vicky Brooker
Consultant: Philip Parker

Picture acknowledgements:
The author and publisher would like to thank the
following agencies and people for allowing these
pictures to be reproduced:

Alamy: North Wind Picture Archives 6, James Boardman
12, World History Archive 16 and 22, Photos 12 17t, The
Art Archive 23b, Granger, NYC. 27t; Dreamstime: Jorisvo
cover tl, 5bl and 25t, Jaime Pharr 23t, Stanzi11 27b;
iStock: james steidl title page l and 4, Chris Mansfield 5t,
jezphotos 5br and 29b, Duncan Walker 9b, duncan1890
13b and 31, Grafissimo 14 and 18, DebbiSmirnoff 19t,
Linda Steward 21b, Paula Connelly 24, Duncan Walker
26, kcline 28, TonyBaggett 29t; Mary Evans Picture
Library: 10 and 25b, Douglas McCarthy 11b, The National
Archives, London. England 17b, Historic England 20;
Rocket Design: 11t; Shutterstock: Peter Lorimer cover tr,
michelaubryphoto cover c, KevinTate cover b, jorisvo title
page r and 13t, Gerhard Roethlinger 7b, Marco Rubino 8,
Pack-Shot 9t, stefbennett 19b, IR Stone 21t; Wikimedia:
Imars: Michael Shea 7t and 32.

All design elements from Shutterstock.

Contents

Who were the Normans?

The Normans built up a powerful duchy in Normandy, France, before conquering England and parts of Italy in the 11th and 12th centuries.

Knights and battles

Fierce knights, skilled archers and clever military tactics helped the Normans win many battles. One of the most important Norman battles was the Battle of Hastings in 1066, in which the Norman army defeated the Anglo-Saxons and killed the king of England. Norman knights also took part in religious wars in the Middle East.

Norman knights wore mail armour and metal helmets. They fought with swords and maces at close range or with lances on horseback.

mace

Brilliant builders

The Normans were skilled builders who put up many large, grand buildings across their lands. Powerful lords lived in wood or stone castles, which were built to help the Normans defend and keep control of their territory. The Normans also built huge cathedrals as a sign of their Christian religion.

The Tower of London was built by the Normans after their conquest of England.

We have learned a lot about the Norman invasion of England from the Bayeux Tapestry, a massive piece of Norman embroidery (see page 25).

How do we know?

We can learn about the history of Normans from artefacts and written records that they left behind. Archaeologists have found Norman weapons, tools and fabric, which help us to understand everyday life in Norman times. Many Norman buildings, such as castles and cathedrals, still stand today across Europe.

This silver coin is from the time of William I, the first Norman king of England. The coin is printed with an image of William's face.

The first Normans

O ver a few centuries, the Normans transformed themselves from Viking raiders to one of the most powerful groups in Europe. Although their religion and language changed, they never lost their fierce fighting spirit.

Viking warriors decorated their longships with carved dragon heads. Norman ships had a similar design.

Viking roots

The first Normans were Vikings from Scandinavia (modern-day Sweden, Denmark and Norway). Between around 800 and the 11th century, fierce Viking warriors sailed from Scandinavia to raid towns and monasteries along the coasts of Scotland, England, Ireland and France.

Becoming Normans

In 911, the Viking warrior Hrolf led an attack on the French town of Chartres. The French offered Hrolf the land around Rouen in exchange for protection against further Viking attacks. Hrolf (later known as Rollo) became the first Viking ruler of Normandy. The French called the Vikings 'Northmen', which turned into 'Normans'.

This modern statue of Hrolf/Rollo is found in the town of Falaise, Normandy.

ROLLON

WALES

ENGLAND

English Channel

NORMANDY

FRANCE

☐ Norman territory from 1066

Over time, the Normans seized more land in northern France. They controlled most of modern-day Normandy.

Jumièges Abbey was destroyed by early Viking raiders, but was later rebuilt by the Norman dukes. Today, only the ruins of the Norman abbey remain.

Powerful rulers

The Normans turned Normandy into one of the most powerful areas in Europe. The ruler of the Normans was given the title 'duke', which was just one rank beneath the king. The Normans integrated well with their French neighbours. They began to speak a version of French, rather than the Scandinavian language, Norse. They gave up the Viking religion and became dedicated Christians.

The rise of the Normans

Once the Normans had secured their duchy in France, they expanded their territory across Europe. They were particularly interested in seizing land in England.

This Norman castle still stands today in Erice, Sicily.

Fighting abroad

Some Norman knights crossed the Mediterranean Sea and conquered land in southern Italy and Sicily. Over time, many Normans settled in these areas and brought the Norman way of life with them. Later, Norman knights took part in the crusades – religious wars between Christians and Muslims over the control of the Holy Land in the Middle East.

The rise of Duke William

In the middle of the 11th century, the French king became worried about the strength of the Normans. He tried to invade Normandy twice, but the Norman duke William defeated him both times. William's victory against the French made him a popular and powerful ruler. He was very ambitious and took every opportunity to expand Norman territory, including north into England.

Today, there is a statue of Duke William in Falaise, Normandy, the town where he was born.

Oaths and loyalty

In 1064, an Anglo-Saxon earl named Harold Godwinson was shipwrecked in Normandy and rescued by William. Norman writers later claimed that Harold swore an oath that he would be loyal to William. William believed that this oath meant that Harold would support William's attempts to become king of England. In January 1066, the Anglo-Saxon king Edward the Confessor died and Harold became king of England. William believed that he was the rightful ruler of England, because of Harold's oath, and so he decided to invade.

According to Norman writers, Harold Godwinson swore an oath of loyalty to Duke William at a special ceremony.

The conquest of England

The Normans weren't the only group that wanted to seize control of England from the Anglo-Saxons. The country also faced attacks in the north from the army of Harald Hardrada, the king of Norway.

Over 10,000 Norwegian and Anglo-Saxons soldiers died at the Battle of Stamford Bridge.

The first attack

Harald Hardrada sailed for England with 300 ships in the autumn of 1066. They landed on the northeast coast and defeated the Anglo-Saxons in that area. Harold Godwinson and his army arrived a few days later and caught Harald by surprise. The Anglo-Saxons defeated the Norwegian army at the Battle of Stamford Bridge and Harald Hardrada was killed.

Moving south

Shortly after defeating Harald Hardrada's army, Harold heard that William had set sail from Normandy with a large army. He marched his army towards the south coast of England. By that point, William had arrived near Pevensey Bay and built camps for his soldiers and a wooden castle.

This map shows how Harold's and William's armies moved towards Hastings.

The Battle of Hastings

On 14 October, William sent his men to attack the Anglo-Saxon army, who were camped on a hill near Hastings. The Anglo-Saxons were at an advantage on the hill, but their soldiers were no match for the Norman knights and archers. After Harold Godwinson was killed in battle, the Normans defeated the Anglo-Saxon army. They marched to London and William was crowned king of England on 25 December 1066.

After William successfully invaded England, he became known as William the Conqueror.

The Battle of Hastings

The Norman and the Anglo-Saxon armies both had a good chance at winning the Battle of Hastings. They were matched in size, with around 8,000 men. Although Harold's men were exhausted after fighting and marching for weeks, the Normans didn't know the land well and had brought limited supplies. Read on to find out how the Battle of Hastings played out and why the Normans were victorious.

On the evening of 13 October 1066, Harold's armies were positioned on top of a hill called Senlac, near Hastings. The Normans were gathered in their camp a few miles away. As the sun set, both armies went to sleep, knowing that tomorrow would bring a day of fighting.

The high-ranking Anglo-Saxon huscarls were armed with long battle-axes and protected by mail armour. Peasant fyrd soldiers wore leather shirts and fought with daggers and spears.

As the sun rose on 14 October, William's army of archers and knights on horseback moved towards the hill. The Anglo-Saxons held their large wooden shields close together, which protected them from the heavy shower of arrows from the Norman archers. William sent foot soldiers and then knights armed with heavy lances to break up the wall of shields, but nothing could get through. The Anglo-Saxons stood strong.

Norman knights tried charging at the enemy at speed, thrusting heavy powerful lances into the line of soldiers.

As the morning went on, a rumour spread across the battlefield that William had been killed. Some Normans began to retreat, followed by Anglo-Saxons who chased the escaping soldiers. William noticed that the Anglo-Saxon wall of shields broke up as they chased the retreating Normans and ordered his men to pretend to retreat again. The Anglo-Saxon wall of shields broke apart and the Normans fought the Anglo-Saxons at close range. By the end of the day, the Normans had defeated the Anglo-Saxons and killed Harold Godwinson.

Some people think that Harold Godwinson may have been hit in the eye by an arrow because it is shown in the Bayeux Tapestry.

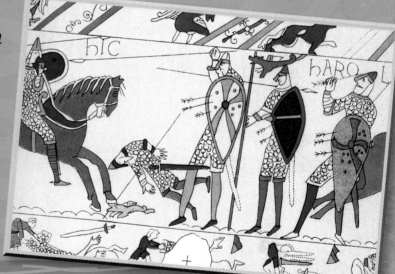

This account has been written for this book, based on the true events of the Battle of Hastings. Can you write the true story of another important Norman battle or event? It could be in England or in another country ruled by the Normans, such as Italy. Use the facts in this book and in other sources to help you write your story.

Make a shield

Norman knights carried long kite-shaped shields into battle. These shields covered most of their bodies while they were on horseback. Norman shields were often decorated with colourful designs and symbols. You can make your own Norman shield from card and create a design for it using coloured pencils.

Norman kite-shaped shields covered most of the body, which meant that it was less important for knights to wear heavy armour on their legs.

You will need:

A3 piece of white card

A4 piece of white paper

coloured pencils or pens

scissors

sticky tape

1 Use scissors to cut a shield shape and a shield handle from the card, as shown in the picture.

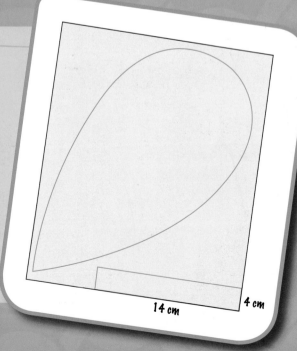

14 cm

4 cm

2 Stick the shield handle to the back of the shield with sticky tape.

3 Practise different shield designs on the piece of white paper. Add colour with the coloured pencils or pens.

4 When you are happy with your shield design, add it to the front of your card shield and colour it in.

Handy hint

Some Norman shield designs and colours had special meanings: a rose symbolised hope, wavy lines meant that a knight lived near the sea and the colour red symbolised a fierce warrior. Do some research into shield designs and design a shield that represents your personality!

Norman society

The Normans had a feudal society, which they copied from the French and brought to the countries that they invaded, such as England.

Feudalism

In feudal countries, the king owned all of the land but let noblemen use it in exchange for loyalty and service in his army. The peasants who lived and worked on a nobleman's land had to pay taxes and fight for their lord in times of war.

Noblemen lived in the castles that the Normans built across England. Peasants lived in huts in the fields around the castles.

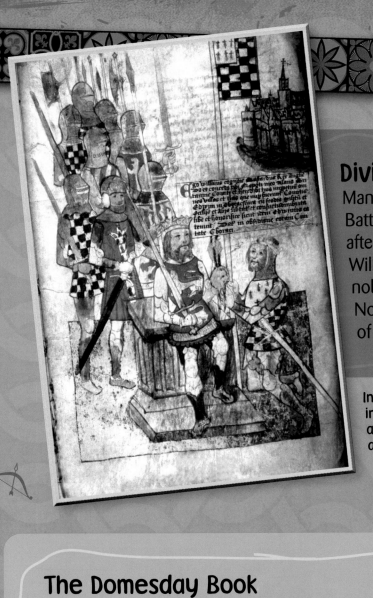

Dividing up land

Many Anglo-Saxon noblemen died at the Battle of Hastings or during rebellions after William became the king of England. William took land away from the Anglo-Saxon noblemen that survived and gave it to Norman lords. The lords were in charge of the peasants that lived on their land.

In this illustration, William is shown giving land in East Anglia and Yorkshire to Alan Rufus, a Norman nobleman who probably fought alongside him at the Battle of Hastings.

The Domesday Book

Twenty years after the Norman conquest, William sent out men to record information about all of the land in England. He wanted to know about every person, village and castle so that he could make sure that the people who lived on his land were paying him enough tax. The information that they gathered was made into the Domesday Book.

We have learned a lot about life in 11th century England from the information in the Domesday Book. We know that most people were peasants and that the noblemen were French-speaking Normans.

Everyday life

Everyday life for the Anglo-Saxons changed after the Norman invasion of England. As well as the new feudal system, the Normans introduced different clothes, foods and language to the lands that they conquered.

Rich Norman women didn't have to do any household work, such as cooking or cleaning, so they could wear fancy clothes made from expensive fabrics and ribbons.

Clothes and fashion

Peasant women wove wool and plant fibres into fabric, which they made into plain, loose clothes for themselves and their families. Rich Norman lords brought new fashions to England from Normandy. Norman women wore fitted dresses with long wide sleeves. Men wore long tunics and cloaks. The Normans in Italy sometimes wore clothes that were influenced by fashions from the Middle East.

Food for all

Most peasants in Norman England ate a simple diet of bread, porridge, soup and occasionally, meat. They grew their own vegetables, such as carrots, onions and cabbages, and raised livestock for milk and wool. Rich Normans ate a wide range of foods, such as meat, fish, fresh fruit, desserts and often held extravagant feasts.

Normans ate stews and soups off of thick slices of bread, which were hollowed out in the centre. These slices of bread, and plates of the same shape, were known as trenchers.

The word 'cow' comes from Old English while the word for its meat, 'beef', comes from Old Norman. This may be because the rich Normans only saw the meat of the cow (beef), while Anglo-Saxon peasants raised the animal, but didn't eat its meat.

A new language

The Normans spoke a version of French that they had learned from the people living around Normandy. They brought their language to England after the invasion and used it for official matters, such as laws and administration. Most of the Anglo-Saxon peasants carried on speaking Old English, the language that they used before the invasion. Over time, the two languages came together to make up the English language that we use today.

Construction and castles

The Normans built grand castles and cathedrals across France, England and Italy, many of which still stand today.

This is an artist's impression of a Norman motte and bailey castle. The steep sides of the motte made it difficult for enemies to get close to the keep.

Castle construction

The Normans quickly built hundreds of castles in England after the conquest to keep control of their new land. The first were simple motte and bailey castles, which had a wooden tower (keep) on top of a mound of earth (motte). People who worked for the lord of the castle lived in an enclosed courtyard called the bailey. The Anglo-Saxons did not build castles, so these massive Norman structures must have been very impressive to them.

keep

bailey

motte

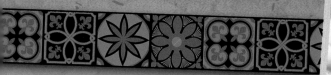

Stone castles

Wooden castles were cheap, quick and easy to build, but they often caught on fire. Over time, the Normans improved their wooden castles and rebuilt some parts in stone. This made the castles much stronger and easier to defend. Many Norman castles also had moats and thick, high walls to slow attackers down.

The Great Keep of Rochester Castle in Kent was built by the Normans in the 1120s. Many parts of the castle still stand today, including its stone keep.

Building in stone

Some Norman buildings in England were built using stone from Normandy. Lords made castles from expensive imported stone as a sign of their wealth. The Normans used boats to transport blocks of stone across the sea and along rivers to the construction site. The stone blocks were moved into place on sledges or by crane. It took between five and ten years to build a stone castle.

Norwich Castle was built from stone that was quarried in Caen, Normandy. The Normans dug a canal near the building site for the ships carrying the stone.

Religion

The Normans were Christians. They took their faith very seriously and made sure that people were practising Christianity across their lands.

Becoming Christians

The first Viking rulers of Normandy followed the Viking religion. They worshipped several gods, including Odin, the king of the gods, and Thor, the god of thunder. Over time, they learned about Christianity from the people living in France and became Christians.

Rollo, the first Viking ruler of Normandy, was baptised as a Christian in 911.

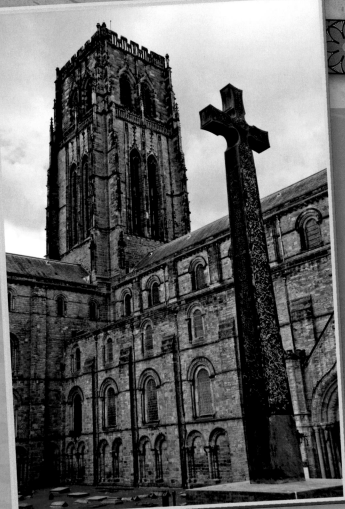

Religious buildings

Norman lords built grand churches, cathedrals and monasteries across England, France and Italy as a sign of their faith and power. In monasteries, monks prayed, studied and made copies of important books. In village churches, Norman priests carried out church services in Latin every Sunday.

The Norman cathedral in Durham, England, still stands today. Some parts of the original Norman cathedral have been rebuilt and added to.

Across land

Some Normans chose to take part in pilgrimages and crusades. In England, pilgrims travelled to holy places, such as Durham and Glastonbury, to touch objects believed to have belonged to saints. Many Normans travelled across Europe to fight in the crusades in the Middle East.

William the Conqueror's eldest son, Robert, fought in the First Crusade from 1096 to 1100.

Art and entertainment

The Normans created beautiful pieces of art, which were often inspired by the crafts of the lands that they conquered.

Influences and inspiration

In England and Normandy, monks made copies of Anglo-Saxon illuminated manuscripts, which were decorated with intricate gold details and illustrations. The Muslims and Byzantines (from an empire based in modern-day Turkey) living alongside the Normans in Italy and Sicily influenced the glass mosaics and patterned walls of Norman cathedrals in Italy.

In England and Normandy, skilled Norman craftsmen often carved patterns and images of people and animals into church columns and doorways.

EXEVNT:CABALLI   DENAVIBVS · - · ET HIC:MILITES · FE

The Bayeux Tapestry

The Bayeux Tapestry is one of the most important pieces of Norman art. This seventy-metre-long piece of embroidery shows the events leading up to and including the Battle of Hastings and was made to celebrate William the Conqueror's victory. Writing in Latin explains the different events and figures.

This image of Norman ships arriving on the coast of England is embroidered in different colours of thread.

Fun at feasts

At feasts, the Normans enjoyed entertainment such as musicians, dancers, actors and jesters. Singers would sing long songs about historical battles or love stories. These entertainers travelled around the country, performing in castles for lords or at village festivals.

A Norman minstrel (singer) performing at a feast. He is playing a lute – a stringed instrument similar to a guitar.

The end of the Normans

Although the Normans were only in power for around 300 years, they made their mark on Europe by conquering large areas of land and building grand castles and cathedrals.

Norman kings of England

After William the Conqueror's death in 1087, William's sons William II (1087–1100) and Henry I (1100–1135) ruled over England. William II and Henry I were well-respected leaders who ruled peacefully. In 1120, Henry I's son and heir died in a shipwreck, so the crown passed to Henry's daughter Matilda when he died.

William II was killed by an arrow while hunting. He was known as William Rufus (meaning red) because his face was very red.

When Henry II married his wife, Eleanor, he gained control of a large area of France.

Civil war

Powerful Normans in England did not want Matilda to rule. They supported Matilda's cousin, Stephen, who seized the throne. This caused a civil war across England and Normandy, which ended with Stephen's death in 1154. The English crown passed to King Henry II, who was Matilda's son and a powerful French noble, and the Norman rule of England ended.

The last Normans

The Normans lost control of Sicily and Italy towards the end of the 12th century. The French took control of Normandy in 1204. Many people who considered themselves Normans married into English or French families, and the Norman identity slowly disappeared. Today, the Normans are remembered as fierce warriors and leaders who had an important impact on the history of Europe.

People enjoy dressing up and re-enacting important events from Norman history, such as the Battle of Hastings.

Facts and figures

The Normans liked to add spices such as ginger, pepper, nutmeg and cardamom to their food. These spices were very expensive because they had to be brought from other countries.

The Normans published books about how to behave at feasts. Guests had to learn where to sit, according to how important they were, and not to behave badly by picking their noses or scratching themselves.

William the Conqueror loved hunting. He made the New Forest in England into a royal forest, where only the king was allowed to hunt.

Henry I, the fourth son of William the Conqueror and king of England from 1100 to 1135, had over twenty five children. He had two or three children with his wife and twenty two to twenty four illegitimate children with different women.

There are 623 people, 202 horses, 55 dogs, 49 trees and 41 ships shown on the Bayeux Tapestry. Of the 623 people, only 3 are women.

The Pope (leader of the Christian church) was unhappy about the large number of people that were killed at the Battle of Hastings, so the Normans built an abbey near the battlefield to show their regret. The ruins of Battle Abbey still stand today.

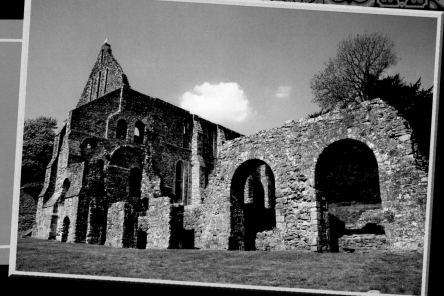

Timeline

CE 911	Viking warrior Rollo is given control of Normandy in exchange for protection against future Viking attacks.
January 1066	Harold Godwinson becomes the king of England.
25 September 1066	Harold Godwinson defeats Harald Hardrada at the Battle of Stamford Bridge.
14 October 1066	William defeats Harold at the Battle of Hastings and begins the Norman conquest of England.
25 December 1066	William is crowned king of England.
1154	King Stephen I, the last Norman king of England, dies.
early 1200s	Norman rulers lose control of Italy and Normandy.

Glossary

administration The work of organising something and making sure it works well

Anglo-Saxon A group of people originally from modern-day Germany and Denmark who ruled over England for several centuries

archaeologists People who learn about the past by digging up old objects

artefact An object from the past that reveals information about the people who made it

CE The letters 'CE' stand for 'common era'. They refer to dates from CE 1.

civil war A war between groups of people who live in the same country

conquer To take control of a country

crusade A religious war fought between Christians and Muslims in the Middle East in the 11th, 12th and 13th centuries

duchy An area of land owned or ruled by a duke or duchess

feudal Describes a system in which the king of a country owns all the land but lets noblemen use it in exchange for their loyalty and service

heir A person who will become king or queen when an older member of their family dies

illegitimate An illegitimate child is born to parents who are not married to each other.

invade To enter a country using force and take control of it

jester A man in the past whose job it was to tell jokes and make people laugh

keep The central, most important tower in a castle

lance A long, pointed weapon used by a knight on horseback when charging towards the enemy

mail Armour made up of thousands of metal rings joined together

moat A long wide pit that is dug around a castle and often filled with water

monastery A building where religious men (monks) live together

nobleman/woman (lord) The richest, most-powerful people in a society, second only to the king

oath A formal promise

peasant A poor person from the past

pilgrimage A journey made for religious reasons

tactics A action that has been planned to help you get what you want

tax Money that you have to pay to the government

territory An area of land that is ruled by a particular leader or group of people

Vikings A group of people originally from Scandinavia who conquered land across northern Europe and the north Atlantic

Further reading

The Battle of Hastings (Why Do We Remember?),
Claudia Martin (Franklin Watts, 2016)

The Battle of Hastings (Great Events),
Gillian Clements (Franklin Watts, 2014)

The Normans and the Battle of Hastings (The History Detective Investigates),
Philip Parker (Wayland, 2012)

Websites

https://www.youtube.com/watch?v=GVMvl05hCrI
Watch a video to see what life was like for 10-year-olds in Norman times.

http://www.bbc.co.uk/schools/primaryhistory/anglo_saxons/normans/includes/ activities/pdfs/a_castle_eye_spy.pdf
Learn how to identify a Norman castle.

http://www.bayeuxtapestry.org.uk
Explore the different scenes on the Bayeux Tapestry.

http://www.english-heritage.org.uk/learn/1066-and-the-norman-conquest/8- factsabout-1066/
Find out eight curious facts about the Battle of Hastings.

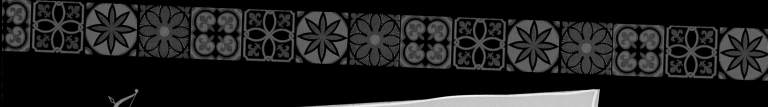

Index